ESTH

MW01595956

Emotional
Creature

Journey Back to Wellness

Esther Rabinovitch

First Edition August 2019

Paperback ISBN: 978-1-08710-829-2

For those who stood by me on my journey through hell.

And for anyone who is going through it right now - don't give up!

Special Thanks to Caroline Nevin.

Esther Rabinovitch

Introduction

The following drawings and poems are a selection of works made from March 2017 to July 2019. They are excerpts from my personal journals, which I started keeping at a time when my life was in shambles.

The journals actually started out as daily gratitude lists in late 2015 - self-prescribed homework logs to challenge the notion that I had nothing to live for, which my mind had been telling me at the time.

Soon after, I started seeing my therapist, and Cognitive Behavioral Therapy exercises were added to my journalling routine to help me combat the notion that *I* was worthless.

And then I started to draw. And draw. And draw.

I decided to be brave and post my drawings to social media, sure that I would be named "impostor" and told that I wasn't good enough...after all, my drawings were never that great in art school and I hadn't done much with my art since graduation. Mercifully, my fears never came to pass. In fact, I received an outpouring of support!

Over time, I also came to the realization that the act of drawing was very meditative and cathartic for me, regardless of whether or not I posted my results online - for the first time in my life, I was creating for myself.

Eventually, words started flowing alongside my drawings. And then independently of the drawings, writing inspiration started to come night and day - it was as if my poems had taken on their own lives, needing to be documented and witnessed.

So here I am, in the Summer of 2019, still healing and working with the arts to get through the challenges and joys of life. Through my work, I have gained strength and a deeper connection with myself and the world around me.

This is the story of my journey back to wellness.

How do I gather in
And offer out?
Paint a clear picture with my words?
If I am delicate
Am I showing my true self?
If I am gentle
Will I be understood?
Questions floating around my mind
About my darkness flowing out
Like an unstoppable, flowing faucet
So I'll just sit and smile
And try to gather in
What hope I can
And offer out
What light I possess

Oh, psychopathology
Disjointed, dynamic pathways
Moving through time and space
Chaotic colour
Moving, always moving
Which way do you want to go?
And what stories do you have to tell?
Disjointed, dynamic pathways
Making space
For transformation

Should, should, should
I should be moving
I should be writing or drawing
Or being compassionate to myself
I should not be judging the experience
I am having in this moment
But I am
I am here
But I am also still breathing
And for now
That's enough

Stings and barbs
Feel what you feel…
I feel like a teenager again
But with the clouding brain of adulthood

Maybe it's not scents you're allergic to…
Perhaps it's me?

Maybe these gatherings carry too much
Generational hurt
Too much trauma

I don't know how to fix this
Broken tradition

You are you
And I am me
We are both flawed
Products of our upbringing
And experiences in life

We are vastly different people
And at once, the same

We both have emotions
That are deeply felt
And we each have
Beating hearts
Beneath our chests

The same issues cause our blood to boil
Even if we have intensely disparate
viewpoints
On more than half of them

We project frustrations onto each other
Ferociously
Without ever meaning harm
Yet causing so much damage
Each spewing our own distinct brand of
venom

Unsure how to stop
Or apologize
Without causing further offense

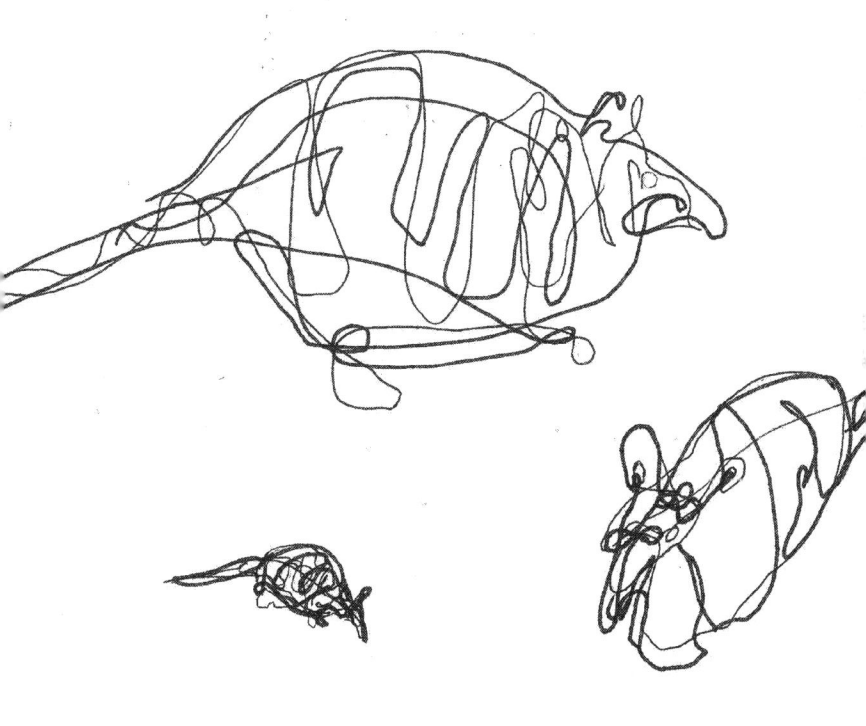

Closure
Endings
When did it end?
Time is fluid
It goes on and on…
Closure…what is closure?
Things end, but I replay the events
The days and moments
Back over in my mind like melodies
Stuck in my head
Haunting and repeating like a spectre
I knew I would miss it before it was even over
And I couldn't maintain my grasp over the days
Sand is less elusive, ice less slippery
Than time

I see you nearly everywhere I go
Especially on the subway
Someone has a haircut
Or jawline
Akin to yours
And it breaks my heart a little
Because it isn't you
I can't walk over and say hi
Or tell him about the funny thing that I saw
that I know you'd love
And I can't help but steal glances at
whoever has your features on a given day
My heart burns - I feel it
Physically feel it
One day…
When I peek across to the stranger on the
train
I dream that there you'll be
In his place
In the same city, at the same time
Smiling in my direction
Welcoming me home

Dipping into the well
Emotions flowing up and around
I'm here for a reason
This is just the beginning
The water runs deep -
Infinite source
I open my mind and move myself
One foot after the other
Legs, torso, arms, neck, and head
This is just the beginning
Infinite source, an abundance of inspiration
Dipping into the well

hands
hands
are
are
weird
weird

I feel beautiful and strong
In my body, in my skin
I feel as though I am getting braver
I feel guided to be more myself,
And it is beautiful
And scary sometimes -
It can be very lonely sometimes,
But rewarding, too
I finally feel as though
I am truly worthy of
Real love, real friendship
And I am ready to let it in
I don't need to change who
Or how I am
I am perfectly imperfect
And though I may not be happy
With every little thing every day and it is
still scary sometimes,
I feel beautiful and strong
In my body

I am alive.
I am still breathing.
That is enough tonight.

My body is my temple
And I am learning how to praise it
How to treat it well and how
To make sacrifices without sacrificing health
I am learning to love my body
And to exalt and rejoice in my form
To see my shape and myself
For the goddess that I am
And always was
My time is now
I am beautiful
I am beauty
I am love

I am proud of my body
Today and all days
For carrying me through
This life
Back and forth, up and down
Back and around
Through traffic
Up and down stairs
Inside, outside
Hot, cold
This body has carried me
Through it all
Always growing
Inside and out
Growing, shrinking, growing, evolving
Always loving and nurturing me
And I am so proud
And grateful

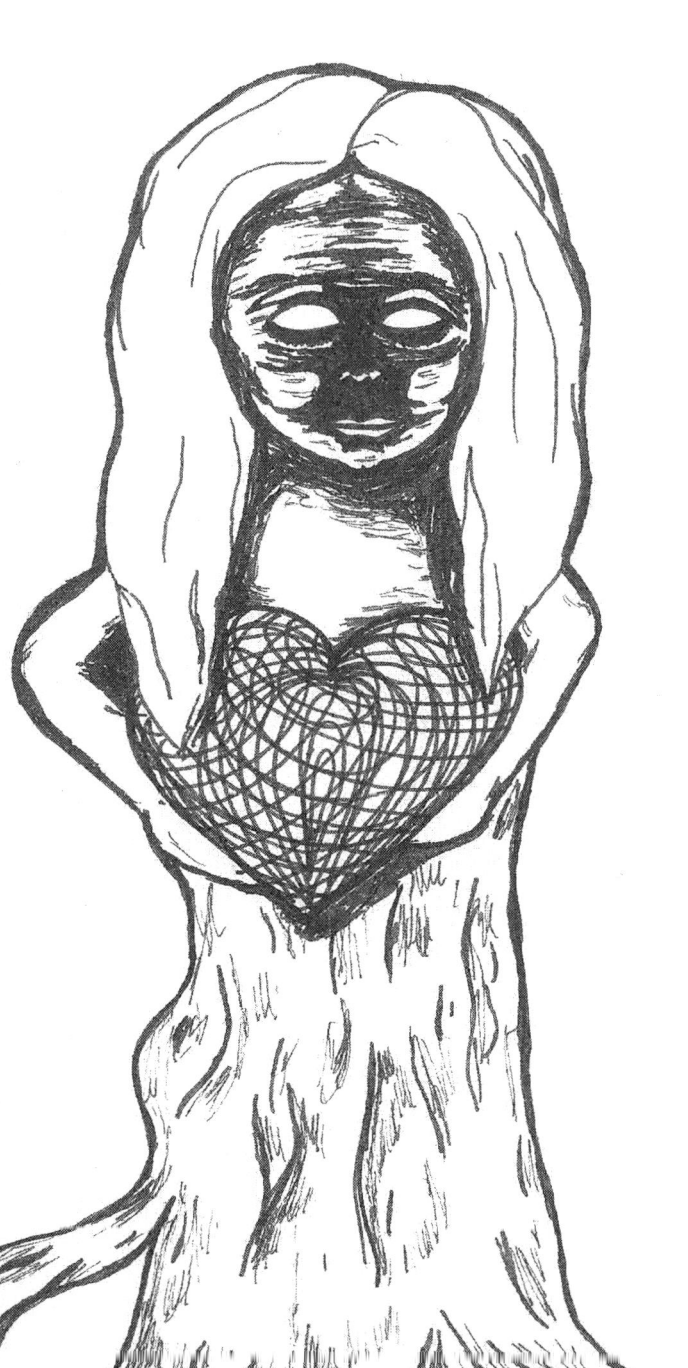

My body aches today
And I honour it by resting
And giving it what it needs
I reschedule plans
I am honest with myself
And others -
I put myself first
For the first time in my life
I feel secure not pushing myself
Finding the balance between
Obligations and kindness
Compassion for self
It is necessary to make space for myself
I am not lazy
I am not a monster
I am healing
I am secure and stable
Within myself
I listen to my body
Even on days when I ache
I slow down and heed the wisdom
In my DNA
I give myself what I need

My body is healing itself
Expelling what no longer serves
It is a visceral process
And can be uncomfortable sometimes
But I am learning to accept
That even in the discomfort
My body is helping me
And working for me
And there is beauty
In the whole journey
I surrender to the process
And embrace all of me
I am grateful to still be here
Learning and loving
And getting braver
With every passing day

Freckles dancing across
My sun-kissed cheeks
Adorning my shoulders
Trickling down my arms
Cascades of tiny beauty marks
Natural tattoos
Marking me a goddess
By the dozen

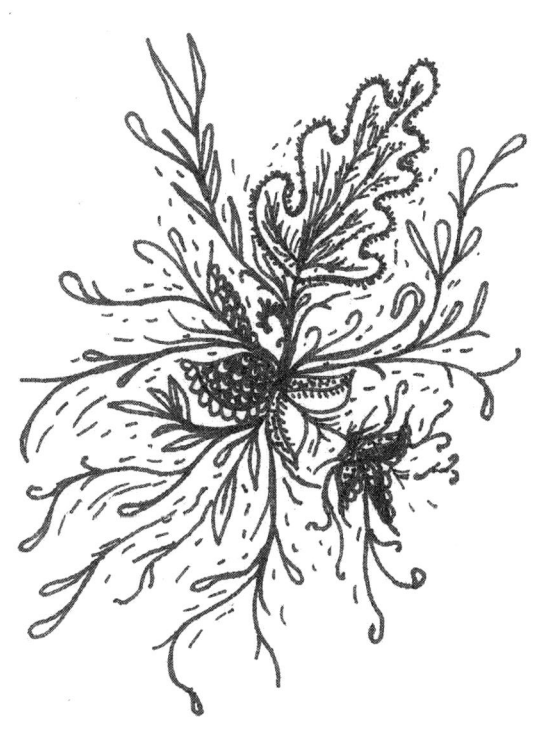

This morning I am weepy
But grateful
For still feeling and living
And functioning
Senses attached to emotions
Working together
I am present
Feeling
Knowing my truth
Experiencing
Myself

I am strong enough
To build the life
That I want to live
I am taking care of my needs
While getting things accomplished
And setting the appropriate boundaries
I am discovering
I am trying
I am enough
I am a badass

I just want
To not be the strong one
For once

I want to be the one
To fall apart

I want permission
To be sad and angry and to cry
Just because

I want to be held
Really held
As I let it all go

I want to be held and seen
Not out of obligation
But out of love
And compassion
And true, mutual companionship

I want to be reassured
And cared for without the burden of worry
At the back of my mind

I just want to be held

Shedding the old, purging what
Doesn't serve, my body aches…
But I know that this is
For the best - this is how
I heal
I am getting better and this
Is the release I've been needing
And craving for literal months
This is my body serving me
This is her way of letting me know
That everything is going to be ok
I am in the flow…
It's all working out…
I'm on the right path
And taking proper care of myself
All is so well and I'm grateful
For this push
And shedding
I am grateful
For my becoming

Out of the ashes of misty gray
You have been reborn
Transformed
The fire burned and cleansed
And here you are, awakened -
Stronger than before…
Don't go back into the mist -
You are here for a reason
Stand your ground, blue wonder
You were meant to rise up
And stand out

I want to participate
In community
But my body says "no"
I screw up and talk in the silent room
Out of sheer nerves
And   worry   that   I'll   make   the   next
presentation run late
It feels like everyone is bombarding me
I don't know which way to turn
I worry that everything I do is wrong
Or somehow offensive
No, it can't be
Can it?
I'm human, too
I'm still worthy
Even when my body and mind say "no"

I want to let my voice stand out
And be reclaimed
But it's scary
The safety of the background
Is the beast I know

I open my mouth to sing
But the sound stays stuck in my throat
I want to dance
But I can only walk
My eyes transfixed
On the ground

I have been here before
Old voices call to me
I am trying to remember the courage and
the joy
That once occupied
This space
The bravery and abandon with which
I would sing and dance and create

Guttural sounds eventually surface -
I want to scream
I want to tear everything beautiful from its
base
I want a do-over
Ashes to ashes

Finally, a hum

"...is she suffering?"

Readying myself some more
Another round
Here we go again
Readying myself
I am steady

***

Sometimes
I can imagine
When I am lucid
An alternate life
I kept up with all my dreams
I see it unfold like a lost vision

***

Who am I
To be so sad
I am grateful
For all that still remains
After all
I am still here

I am solid
Steady in myself
Travelling through centuries
Softening
And absorbing light
A grounding force
Forged from the depths of the fiery Earth

I wanted to tell you
How much it meant
All those summers and March breaks
In St. Laurent
Running up green, carpeted stairs
Looking at old photos
Chatting in the kitchen
And watching
As you cooked the Friday evening
kneidlach
I can still hear your voices
Like lullabies
I meant to visit more often
I did not tell you then
But if I had the chance
I would tell you now
I have not forgotten you

By the Detroit River
We thought time would stand still -
Has age got you down?

... sometimes unravelling
is the answer

Trust the process - ha!
Over-thinking is how I
Always operate…

I feel stretched thin like an eel
Trying to pass through unscathed
Electrified by my own thoughts
But I am still hopeful as a newborn
Learning acceptance each day
These are not foreign waters

My mom's eyes are playing tricks
And the Notre-Dame Cathedral is on fire
Rain's internal organs are failing her
One by one…

Something is telling me to keep my head up
And that things will get better

My mom will recover
The Cathedral in France is just a building
Rain's a fighter

It's only Monday

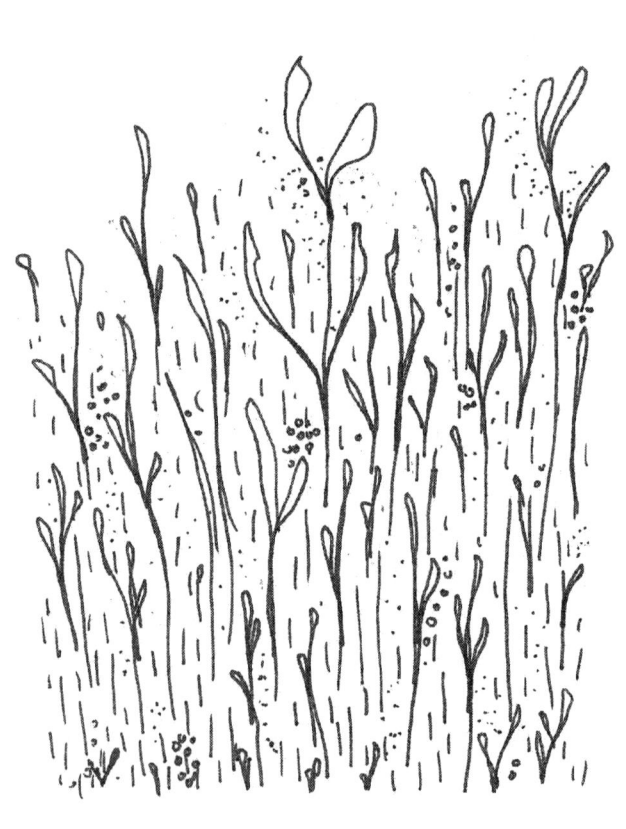

And they looked at me
With wide eyes
Was it sadness or blankness
I saw there?
Maybe one of each?
They looked at me
And asked -
Is there anything you need
From us in this moment?
INTEGRITY.
ACCOUNTABILITY.
CRITICAL THOUGHT.
Still shaking, I tell them
No, I'll figure it out
This is not the first time
This witch has burned

Spiraling out
Cobblestone brain
Something's gotta give
So this is Compassion Fatigue

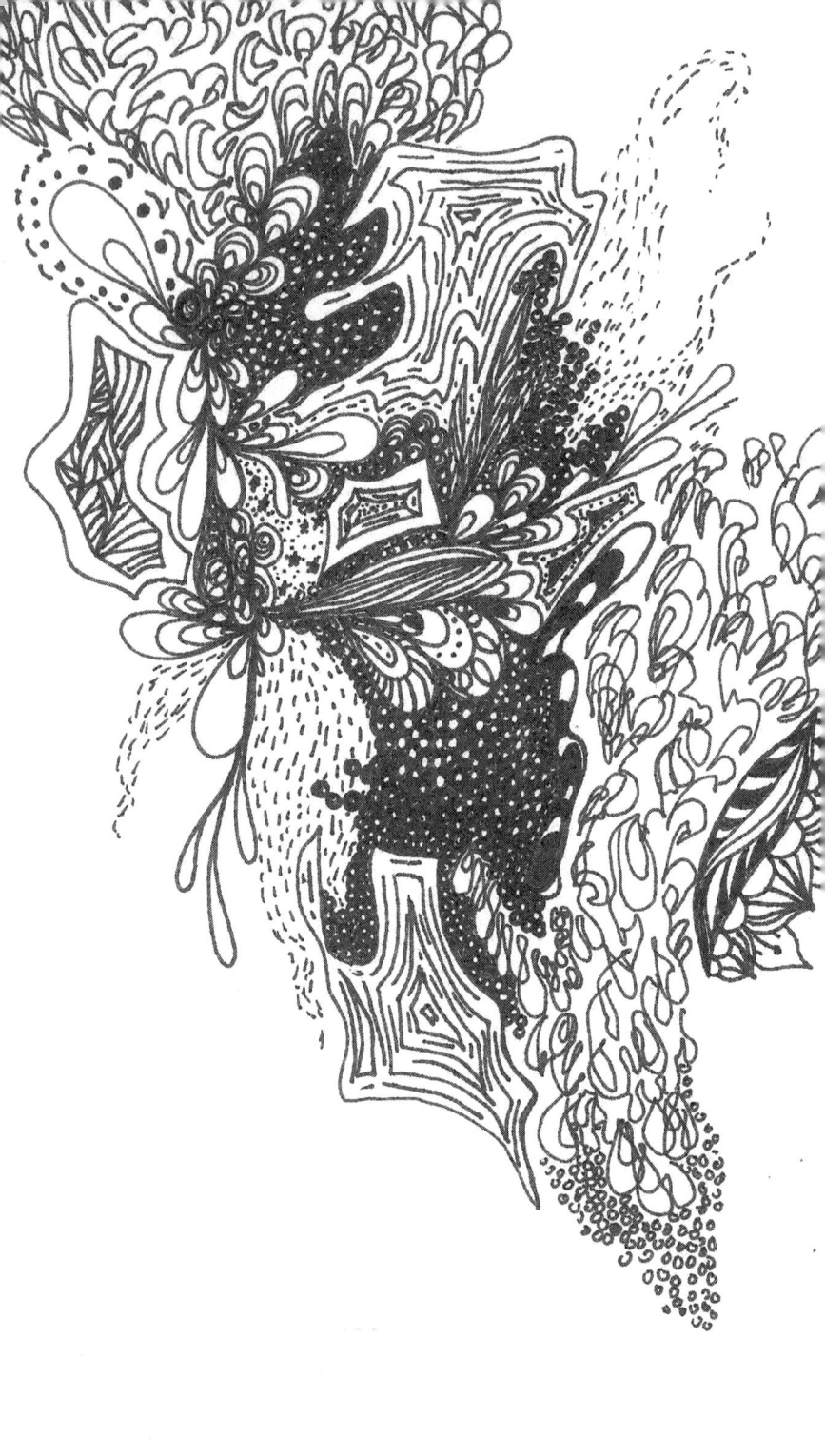

I live with disability
And struggle with chronic pain
This does not make me broken
Or less whole
Than anybody else
It has taken me years to come to terms
With the person living in this skin
I can feel beautiful on days
That I flare
And defeated on days that I function
...like everybody else
I am no less
And no more
Than anybody else

Early morning blues
Still awake, I start to sing
Sitting on the can

When the treatment is worse than the
condition,
Side effects abound -
Bruising, burning, writhing...
This is the less invasive option,
I am assured
Just be compliant - what's a few more
months,
After a couple decades
Of likely misdiagnosis?
Bruising, bloating, writhing
I burn -
Why the fuck are we so far from
understanding
Women's health?

I think that I knew
That emotional pain
Manifests itself in the physical body
Long before reading Mate or van der Kolk

As a girl
I used to scratch my hands
Until they bled
If I was nervous, angry, or scared
Which I often was

I developed asthma and gastritis and couldn't sleep
And was told I was depressed and anxious before adolescence

I was awkward and bullied and felt embarrassed and ashamed
Most of the time

I almost died from an illness of the liver at nineteen
After being physically assaulted the year prior
And tried to drink myself into oblivion at twenty

And on and on and on

Cycles of abuse, blame, and shame

Tear through me now
Sober
Calm
Sensitive
Angry, but still here

My body keeps score with a vengeance

Process, feel, heal

Red, hot
Older than me
If I'm not careful
You'll burn me to the core
But, in this moment, you're
Essential to my
Survival

I want to take a leap…
And I know that it's in an unpopular
direction…
I want to move away from what I've been
building toward
And land in authenticity somewhere
That resonates with my soul
I want to create
I want to live my life crafting things that I
am passionate about
I don't want to struggle or to feel like
I am working so hard all of the time
For scraps
I want to spend my days
Growing
Loving
Being
I want to take the leap…
I want to succeed on my own terms

Every six months or so
I use this yellow, numbing cream
A chemical brew
Of all the painkillers that can fit into a fifty
Gram dispenser
Taken orally, I imagine the combination might
Be lethal
Applied topically, I get a short burst of sweet
Relief
I often forget that this concoction is an option
And something I have at my disposal
Frightfully expensive and with effects that are
Often short-lived
I don't even recall that it exists in my ownership
Most of the time
On the rare occasion that I do remember, I am
Grateful for the pharmaceutical marvel that is
This golden, wonder brew
Stashed for months
Forgotten in the depths of my bureau
Tonight, I remember
I choose to be gentle with myself

Generously dispensing the calming goop into
My gloved hand
Massaging the discomfort from my aching body
Breathing a sigh of relief as the pain melts
From my hip and leg
My pulse slows
And I try not to worry how long this will last
And look forward, instead, to a peaceful night
Of sleep
Stashing the white, prescription bottle back in its place
To be forgotten

For years I felt as though my life had no meaning
Every moment awake was a moment spent
Drifting, aimless
I chose to close my eyes
and escape myself
I tried to hide who I was and stay asleep
And all I got for my effort was pain
An abundance of pain
Then, something in me snapped
I started to open up
And let people in
I had to let my true self out
And now
Years into wading through all of my emotional
Shtick
I finally feel fully open
In touch with my truths and in harmony with
Who I am
I wake early and stay up late
My joie de vivre has returned
And I notice the outpouring of love from those
Who surround me
I can still become overwhelmed sometimes by
The outside world
But I am aware of all the beauty

And grateful for all of the joy and support and
Compassion
I will not return to my haze
I choose to be a participant in life
I recognize that my life has always been
Meaningful
I choose to stay awake

No time
No distance
No man, woman, or thing
From above
Or below
Can shift my perspective
I cannot be swayed
You have my whole heart
Outside influences be damned
Our love is not a curse
It's the cure
It's destiny
I cannot be swayed
From this knowing

Today
My mother and I try out armchairs
To add more comfort to my experience
Overpriced, modern, tacky
We giggle and take stock of the many
Salespeople with medical degrees
As they spot me with my cane
Suggesting that I sleep on hardwood floors
And purchase their priciest wing-backed
chaises -
Obvious cures for what ails me
Back at the car, Mum and I plan our
pilgrimage
To Ikea

Weekly
I attend to pain management
Soft-tissue   massage,   chiropractic
adjustments,
And electrostim-acupuncture
Numb my spine
As I chat with my doctor about superheroes
And *Stranger Things*

Occasionally
I kick it up a notch
Cortisone injections
Calm my irritated nerves
The pungent stench of rubbing alcohol
stings my nose

As I joke with nurses about the crazy
weather
We've been having
And smile to myself
As the anesthesiologist queues up house
beats
To listen to as he conducts my procedure

Rarely
I burst into tears
Dejected, hopeless, furious with my body
As I pity myself
And turn to YouTube for distraction
Mukbangs on *Hot Ones* -
Oh, the schadenfreude!
Suddenly things don't seem so bad

Always
I find silver linings
Reasons to laugh and smile
Pain is pain
And it can be shitty
But there is joy all around me
And guacamole in my fridge

I refuse
To be limited
Or restricted
By my pain
I choose to turn it
Somehow
Into gold

If these are my cards
Then I call the universal bluff
I see now my purpose
In manifesting success
I'm going to play the hell out of my hand

I choose
To turn my situation
From sorrow
Into gold
And somehow
Rise up from these
Ashes

There are friendships
That have bled me dry
There are people who energetically take and
drain
Wanting for others to stay small
So that they can feel more established and
safe

I've had to release these beings from my life
To regain my sense of self
To retain my sanity
And maintain my self-worth

These individuals come back from time to
time
Probing for my secrets to success
Attempting to mine me
For their own personal gain
Assuming my ignorance to their parasitic
ways

But here's the thing
From my perspective
To truly succeed:

Be kind
Create with passion

Look in the mirror and and take an honest
assessment of yourself

Be kind some more
Show up for what sets you on fire

Be kind
And be brave enough
To walk away from those
Who are not

I am an
Emotional creature
A vulnerable, spiritual
Being

I love hard
And rage
Fiercely

The creature is not
Separate from me

I am steady and stable
I hold my darkness
As a friend
I become the alchemist

I rise up
Again and again
An emotional creature

Unbroken

You Matter.

You are enough.

You are not alone.

♡ esther

ESTHER RABINOVITCH is an artist based in Stouffville, Canada. *Emotional Creature* is her first collection of poetry and drawings. It was crafted all over Southwestern Ontario and in the wee hours of the morning.

Made in the USA
Middletown, DE
19 January 2020